United States Government Accountability Office

GAO

Report to the Committee on Homeland Security and Governmental Affairs, U.S. Senate

I0415785

July 2012

CHIEF ACQUISITION OFFICERS

Appointments Generally Conform to Legislative Requirements, but Agencies Need to Clearly Define Roles and Responsibilities

GAO

Accountability ★ Integrity ★ Reliability

GAO-12-792

Highlights of GAO-12-792, a report to the Committee on Homeland Security and Governmental Affairs, U.S. Senate

July 2012

CHIEF ACQUISITION OFFICERS

Appointments Generally Conform to Legislative Requirements, but Agencies Need to Clearly Define Roles and Responsibilities

Why GAO Did This Study

Federal agencies spent more than half a trillion dollars in fiscal year 2011 through contracts to acquire goods and services in support of their missions, but have historically faced significant acquisition management challenges preventing them from getting the best return on their investments. The SARA legislation requires 16 federal civilian agencies to appoint a Chief Acquisition Officer to advise and assist agency leadership to help ensure that the agency's mission is achieved through the management of its acquisition activities. GAO was asked to examine: (1) how agencies have filled the CAO position; (2) the extent to which CAOs are involved in performing the acquisition management functions set forth in the SARA legislation and Office of Management and Budget (OMB) guidance; and (3) what challenges, if any, agency CAOs report in fulfilling their responsibilities. GAO administered a questionnaire to 16 CAOs, reviewed documentation on CAOs' roles and responsibilities, organizational placement, and backgrounds, and interviewed a number of CAOs and other acquisition officials.

What GAO Recommends

GAO recommends that the Administrator of OMB's Office of Federal Procurement Policy work with the CAO Council to issue guidance directing agencies to more clearly define CAOs' roles and responsibilities. The Administrator agreed with the recommendation.

View GAO-12-792. For more information, contact William T.Woods at (202) 512-4841 or WoodsW@gao.gov.

What GAO Found

Most agencies have appointed Chief Acquisition Officers (CAO) in accordance with two of the three key requirements in the Services Acquisition Reform Act of 2003 (SARA): that the CAOs be political appointees and have agency Senior Procurement Executives report directly to them. However, few CAOs have acquisition management as their primary duty; other areas of responsibility included financial, information, and human capital management.

CAO Characteristics

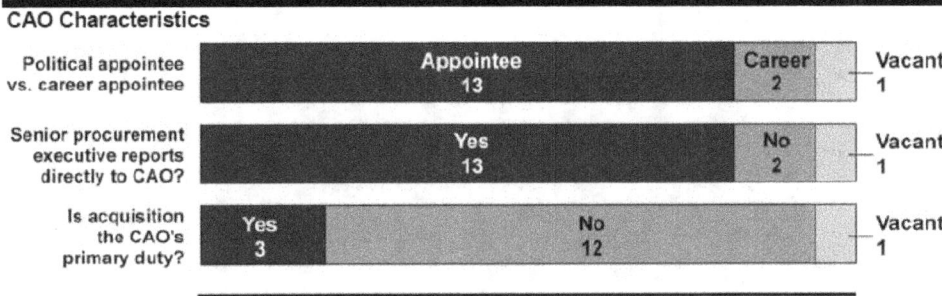

Political appointee vs. career appointee	Appointee 13	Career 2	Vacant 1
Senior procurement executive reports directly to CAO?	Yes 13	No 2	Vacant 1
Is acquisition the CAO's primary duty?	Yes 3	No 12	Vacant 1

Number of CAOs (16 total under SARA)

Source: GAO analysis of CAO survey.

Several CAOs noted that their additional responsibilities were not a detriment. Rather, they believe that performing multiple roles helps them positively influence acquisition management across their agencies. For example, the CAO at the Department of Commerce stated that his additional responsibilities gave him the ability to integrate planning, budgeting, risk management, human resources, and acquisition to achieve the agency's mission.

CAOs reported varying levels of involvement in the acquisition management functions for which they are responsible. Generally, CAOs see their role as providing high-level oversight of the acquisition function as opposed to day-to-day management, which they typically delegated to the Senior Procurement Executive or other officials as permitted by the legislation. Many CAOs said that the amount of their involvement is related to several factors, such as the nature of goods and services that the agency buys and whether the agency has a centralized or decentralized acquisition function.

Having clearly defined roles and responsibilities of stakeholders in the acquisition process is a key element of an effective acquisition function. Yet at many agencies, the statutory roles and responsibilities of the CAO position are not described in detail in acquisition regulations, policies, or other documentation. These agencies may be missing an opportunity to fully institutionalize the CAO position within their senior leadership structures.

CAOs at the 16 agencies generally did not report facing significant challenges related to the CAO position, such as the level of influence they have in their agency's acquisition process, amount of control over acquisition budget resources, and access to agency leadership. Consistent with our prior work on the acquisition workforce, however, most CAOs reported that not having enough staff to manage acquisitions was moderately to extremely challenging.

_____ **United States Government Accountability Office**

Contents

Abbreviations

CAO	Chief Acquisition Officer
CFO	Chief Financial Officer
CHCO	Chief Human Capital Officer
CIO	Chief Information Officer
DHS	Department of Homeland Security
EPA	Environmental Protection Agency
FAR	Federal Acquisition Regulation
GSA	General Services Administration
HHS	Department of Health and Human Services
HUD	Department of Housing and Urban Development
IG	Inspector General
IT	information technology
NASA	National Aeronautics and Space Administration
OFPP	Office of Federal Procurement Policy
OMB	Office of Management and Budget
SARA	Services Acquisition Reform Act of 2003
.SPE	Senior Procurement Executive
VA	Department of Veterans Affairs

United States Government Accountability Office
Washington, DC 20548

July 26, 2012

The Honorable Joseph I. Lieberman
Chairman
The Honorable Susan M. Collins
Ranking Member
Committee on Homeland Security and Governmental Affairs
United States Senate

In fiscal year 2011, federal agencies collectively spent more than half a trillion dollars through contracts to acquire goods and services in support of their missions. With the United States facing increasing fiscal pressures, there is a need to ensure that federal agencies make the most efficient and effective use of their resources. However, agencies have historically faced significant acquisition management challenges that have prevented them from getting the best return on their investments in goods and services. To address these challenges, agencies must establish a strong foundation for an effective, efficient and accountable acquisition process, which includes proper organizational alignment and committed agency leadership. To this end, the Services Acquisition Reform Act of 2003 (SARA)[1] requires 16 federal civilian agencies to establish the position of a Chief Acquisition Officer (CAO) to advise and assist agency leadership to help ensure that the agency's mission is achieved through the management of its acquisition activities.

You asked that we review the implementation of the CAO position at federal agencies. In response, we examined: (1) how agencies have filled the CAO position; (2) the extent to which CAOs are involved in performing the acquisition management functions set forth in the SARA legislation and Office of Management and Budget (OMB) guidance, and (3) what challenges, if any, agency CAOs report in fulfilling their responsibilities. To address these objectives, we analyzed the SARA legislation and directives from OMB's Office of Federal Procurement Policy (OFPP) to identify the key roles and responsibilities of the CAO position. We then

---

[1] Pub. L. No. 108-136, § 1421, 117 Stat. 1663 (codified as amended at 41 U.S.C. § 1702).

administered a questionnaire by e-mail to the 16 civilian agencies[2] within the scope of our review.[3] The questionnaire requested information on, among other things, the CAOs' organizational reporting relationships, tenure, involvement in acquisition management functions within the agency, and challenges experienced in fulfilling their CAO responsibilities. We received responses from all 16 agencies, though not all agencies provided responses to each question. We also collected and reviewed agency organizational charts, acquisition regulations and guidance, applicable policies and delegation orders, as well as biographical information, to identify the organizational placement, roles and responsibilities, and professional background of the CAO position within the agency. Finally, we conducted follow-up interviews to discuss the CAO's roles and responsibilities with CAOs and acquisition officials at seven agencies: Energy, the General Services Administration (GSA), Commerce, Department of Health and Human Services (HHS), Interior, Department of Homeland Security (DHS), and the National Aeronautics and Space Administration (NASA). We selected a nongeneralizable sample of agencies for follow-up interviews based upon the following criteria: review of the questionnaire responses, the agency's procurement obligations in fiscal year 2010, and whether the agency's Inspector General had identified acquisition-related issues as a major management challenge. Our review did not assess the effectiveness of individual CAOs or individual agencies' acquisition functions. A more complete description of our objectives, scope, and methodology is provided in appendix I.

We conducted this performance audit from October 2011 to July 2012 in accordance with generally accepted government auditing standards. Those standards require that we plan and perform the audit to obtain sufficient, appropriate evidence to provide a reasonable basis for our findings and conclusions based on our audit objectives. We believe that

---

[2] We sent the questionnaire to the Departments of Agriculture, Commerce, Education, Energy, Health and Human Services, Homeland Security, Housing and Urban Development, the Interior, Labor, State, Transportation, the Treasury, Veterans Affairs, the Environmental Protection Agency, the National Aeronautics and Space Administration, and the General Services Administration (GSA).

[3] The SARA legislation exempts the Department of Defense (DOD) from the CAO requirement. Legislation enacted prior to SARA required DOD to have an Under Secretary of Defense (Acquisition, Technology & Logistics) who has responsibilities similar to those of a CAO. Justice is not required to appoint a CAO under the SARA legislation, but has designated the Assistant Attorney General for Administration as the CAO.

GAO-12-792 Chief Acquisition Officers

the evidence obtained provides a reasonable basis for our findings and conclusions based on our audit objectives.

Background

Chief Acquisition Officers provide a focal point for acquisition in agency operations. The SARA legislation requires that CAOs:

- be noncareer employees;[4]
- have acquisition management as their primary duty; and
- have the agency's Senior Procurement Executive (SPE) report directly to them without intervening authority, or serve as both CAO and SPE.[5]

The SARA legislation outlined seven acquisition management functions CAOs are expected to perform within their agencies. Subsequent to the enactment of SARA, governmentwide directives and guidance have assigned CAOs responsibility for additional functions, such as internal control reviews of the acquisition function under OMB Circular A-123 and ensuring the quality of federal procurement data. The key functions of the CAO we reviewed are listed below; additional information on these functions is also available in appendix II:

- monitoring and evaluating agency acquisition activities;
- increasing the use of full and open competition;
- increasing performance-based contracting;
- making acquisition decisions;
- managing agency acquisition policy;
- acquisition career management;
- acquisition resources planning; and
- conducting acquisition assessments under OMB Circular A-123.

The SARA legislation also established a Chief Acquisition Officers Council that is chaired by OMB's Deputy Director for Management, and

---

[4] For purposes of this report, we refer to noncareer employees as political appointees. For additional information, see GAO, *Personnel Practices: Conversions of Employees from Political to Career Positions May 2005-May 2009*, GAO-10-688 (Washington, D.C.: June 28, 2010).

[5] The Senior Procurement Executive position was established in 1983 prior to the creation of the CAO position (see Pub. L. No. 98-191, § 7). The Senior Procurement Executive is typically a career employee who is responsible for management direction of an agency's procurement system, including implementation of the agency's unique procurement policies, regulations, and standards.

GAO-12-792 Chief Acquisition Officers

whose activities are led by the OFPP Administrator.[6] The council is the principal interagency forum for monitoring and improving the federal acquisition system. Its activities include developing recommendations for the Director of OMB on acquisition policies and requirements; sharing best practices; and helping to address the hiring, training, and professional development needs of the acquisition workforce.

Our prior work has emphasized the need for strong, effective leadership and the appropriate placement of the acquisition function within agencies among many key factors needed in order to facilitate efficient, effective, and accountable acquisition processes. Clear, strong, and ethical executive leadership, including a CAO, is key to obtaining and maintaining organizational support for executing the acquisition function.[7] Most of the agencies required to appoint a CAO spend a substantial amount of funding each year through contracts to acquire goods and services in support of their missions, as shown below in table 1. Yet, acquisition management challenges persist among many of these agencies. Among the 16 agencies, 11 had acquisition-related issues identified as a major management challenge by their respective Inspector General (IG) in its most recent report on agency management challenges. Additionally, our high-risk list includes a number of areas related to acquisition management.[8]

---

[6] Pub. L. No. 108-136, § 1422, 117 Stat. 1663, 1668 (2003).

[7] GAO, *Framework for Assessing the Acquisition Function at Federal Agencies*, GAO-05-218G (Washington, D.C.: Sept. 2005).

[8] GAO, *High-Risk Series: An Update*, GAO-11-278 (Washington, D.C.: Feb. 2011).

Table 1: CAO Agencies' Contract Spending and Acquisition Management Challenges

Agency	Fiscal year 2011 funded contract obligations (in billions)	Contract obligations as percentage of agency fiscal year 2011 discretionary budget authority	Acquisition-related issues identified as a major management challenge by agency IG
Energy	$21.3	82.9%	X
HHS	$19.9	25.8%	X
Veterans Affairs	$17.8	31.5%	X
DHS	$14.8	35.1%	X
NASA	$14.7	79.7%	X
State	$9.2	35.2%	X
GSA	$7.1	Not applicable	X
Treasury	$7.0	52.0%	
Agriculture	$5.4	23.3%	
Transportation	$4.9	28.9%	X
Commerce	$3.2	56.8%	X
Interior	$3.0	25.7%	
Labor	$2.5	20.1%	X
Environmental Protection Agency	$2.1	24.2%	
Education	$1.9	2.8%	X
Housing and Urban Development	$1.8	4.8%	

Source: GAO analysis of federal procurement data, OMB historical budget data, and Inspector General reports.

Note: GSA primarily funds its operations through fee revenue generated by its activities, as opposed to the use of appropriated funds.

Since the creation of the CAO position, other reviews have made recommendations related to its implementation at specific agencies:

- The Department of Labor IG has frequently reported on concerns that the agency has not been in compliance with the SARA requirement for the CAO to have acquisition management as the primary duty.
- A 2011 Department of Transportation IG report also found that the department's acquisition organizational structure does not effectively support the department's acquisition function, and noted that the CAO does not have acquisition management as the primary duty.

Agencies Have Established CAOs as a Focal Point for Acquisition, but Most Have Other Management Responsibilities and Short Tenures

The agencies within the scope of our review generally have established CAOs in a way that satisfies two of three key aspects of the legislation. The CAOs in place at these agencies are generally political appointees situated at top levels in their organization, and at most agencies, the Senior Procurement Executive reports directly to the CAO. However, very few agency CAOs have acquisition management as their primary duty, the third key requirement of the SARA legislation. Most of these CAOs have other significant management responsibilities within their agencies, such as serving as the Chief Financial Officer (CFO). Additionally, some CAOs and acquisition officials said it was a challenge in determining how to fill the position within their agency, because the SARA legislation did not provide an additional leadership slot specifically for the CAO position. Tenure in the CAO position also has been relatively short, as the average CAO tenure was about 2 years, and several agencies have had frequent turnover in CAOs.

CAOs Generally Appointed in Accordance with Requirements, but Few Have Acquisition Management as Their Primary Duty

As shown below in figure 1, most agency CAOs are political appointees and have the Senior Procurement Executives report directly to them, but few have acquisition management as their primary duty.

Figure 1: CAO Characteristics

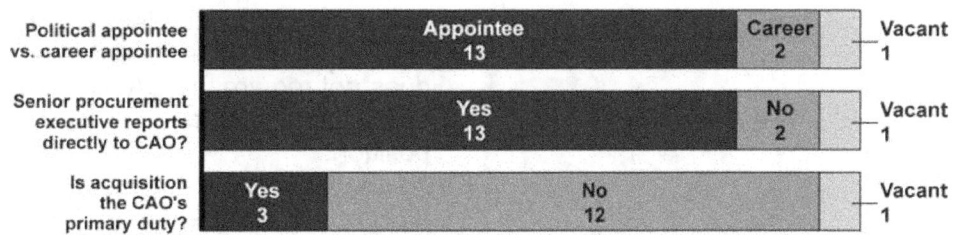

Number of CAOs (16 total under SARA)

Source: GAO analysis of CAO survey.

- Twelve of the 16 agencies had a permanent CAO in place at the time we administered our questionnaire.[9] Three agencies (Education, Department of Veterans Affairs (VA) and Department of Housing and Urban Development (HUD)) had an acting CAO, and the position was vacant at Energy, which is currently relying on the Senior Procurement Executive as its lead acquisition official.[10] All 12 permanent CAOs were political appointees, and 1 of the 3 acting CAOs was a political appointee.
- At 13 agencies, the Senior Procurement Executive reports directly to the Chief Acquisition Officer without intervening authority. The Senior Procurement Executive does not report directly to the CAO at 2 agencies—HHS and NASA. Officials at these agencies told us there is an informal reporting relationship between the two positions. HHS also noted that despite the indirect organizational relationship between the two positions, the CAO and Senior Procurement Executive communicate frequently on the department's acquisition policies, priorities, and programs.
- Only 3 of the CAOs in place during our review (DHS, GSA, and VA) reported that acquisition management was their primary duty, another requirement of the SARA legislation. When asked to estimate the amount of time spent on their CAO duties relative to their other

---

[9] Following the administration of our CAO questionnaire, 3 agencies reported changes in the CAO position. The GSA CAO left the agency in April 2012. GSA appointed an acting CAO in June 2012 who also serves as Senior Advisor to the Acting Administrator. The Treasury CAO also left the agency in April 2012 and the position is held by an acting official who is a political appointee. HUD, which had an acting CAO at the time we administered our questionnaire, now has a permanent CAO who is a political appointee.

[10] In the past, Energy's CAO has been a political appointee to whom the SPE directly reported, and has had acquisition management as the primary duty.

responsibilities, the average among the 14 agencies that provided a response was about 27 percent. Furthermore, only 3 of the 12 permanent CAOs in place during our review had prior experience in acquisition or procurement prior to serving as CAO. Although SARA does not require the CAO to have a background in acquisition, this is one of many factors that could affect the CAO's success in the position.

- As shown below in table 2, almost all of the CAOs in our review had additional management responsibilities and few had an official title of Chief Acquisition Officer. For example, at the Departments of State, Agriculture, and Commerce, the Assistant Secretary for Administration serves as the CAO. These officials' additional areas of responsibility, among other things, include financial management, information management, equal employment opportunity, and emergency preparedness.

Table 2: Official Titles and Management Responsibilities of Chief Acquisition Officers

Agency	Official title of the Chief Acquisition Officer	Number of additional positions held within agency (excluding official title)	Chief Acquisition Officer also serves as the		
			Chief Financial Officer	Chief Human Capital Officer	Chief Information Officer
Agriculture	Assistant Secretary for Administration	0			
Commerce	Chief Financial Officer/Assistant Secretary for Administration	5	X	X	
DHS	Under Secretary for Management	0			
Education	Chief Financial Officer	1	X		
Energy	Chief Acquisition Officer (vacant)	0			
EPA	Assistant Administrator	4		X	
GSA	Chief Acquisition Officer	0			
HHS	Assistant Secretary for Financial Resources	5	X		
HUD	Deputy Secretary	3			
Interior	Assistant Secretary, Policy, Management and Budget	7	X	X	
Labor	Assistant Secretary for Administration and Management	2		X	X
NASA	Chief Financial Officer	2	X		
State	Assistant Secretary for Administration	4			
Transportation	Deputy Secretary	1			

Agency	Official title of the Chief Acquisition Officer	Number of additional positions held within agency (excluding official title)	Chief Acquisition Officer also serves as the		
			Chief Financial Officer	Chief Human Capital Officer	Chief Information Officer
Treasury	Assistant Secretary for Management, Chief Financial Officer and Chief Performance Officer	2	X		
VA	Principal Executive Director, Office of Acquisition, Logistics and Construction	0			

Source: GAO analysis of agency information

Although acquisition management is supposed to be a CAO's primary duty, several CAOs we met with told us that having responsibility for additional management functions was not a detriment and often helped them positively influence acquisition management across their agency:

- At half of the 16 agencies, the Chief Acquisition Officer also serves in at least one additional "Chief" officer position. Similar to the SARA legislation, the legislation that created the Chief Human Capital Officer (CHCO) and Chief Information Officer (CIO) positions required that those respective functions be the primary duty of each position.[11] We have raised concerns in prior work about those positions having additional significant responsibilities and whether an individual serving in these positions can deal effectively with an agency's management challenges.[12] Although this could be a concern with respect to CAOs who do not have acquisition management as their primary duty, the Office of Federal Procurement Policy noted that an agency's Senior Procurement Executive provides high-level attention to the management of the acquisition function.
- Some CAOs and acquisition officials also pointed out that the SARA legislation did not provide agencies an additional position specifically for the CAO, which created a challenge for agencies to determine how to fill the CAO position. For example, the NASA CAO noted in her

---

[11] Chief Human Capital Officers Act of 2002, Pub .L. No. 107-296, § 1302, 116 Stat. 2287, 2288; Information Technology Management Reform Act of 1996, Pub. L. No. 104-106, § 5125, 110 Stat. 679, 684.

[12] GAO, *Human Capital: Observations on Agencies' Implementation of the Chief Human Capital Officers Act*, GAO-04-800T (Washington, D.C.: May 18, 2004); and *Chief Information Officers: Ensuring Strong Leadership and an Effective Council*, GAO/T-AIMD-98-22 (Washington, D.C.: Oct. 27, 1997).

questionnaire response that the agency has a low allocation of politically appointed positions. As a result, NASA gave the CAO duties to the CFO. NASA's CAO stated that because the agency spends such a large amount of its budget through obligations on contracts, her role as the CFO is closely connected with her additional role as the CAO to effectively conduct acquisition management at NASA. Furthermore, the NASA CAO thought that having these two functions integrated was a positive aspect of her current position and helped her be an effective CAO, as opposed to having acquisition operate in a separate stovepipe.

- The CAO at Commerce emphasized the positive aspects of the agency's organizational structure and approach to implementation of the CAO position. At Commerce, one individual serves in a number of roles that includes the CFO, CHCO, and Chief Performance Officer as well as the CAO. The CAO noted that this structure gave him the ability to integrate planning, budgeting, risk management, human resources, as well as acquisition to achieve the agency's mission. As the individual who ties these functional areas together, he indicated he has the authority to get other groups within Commerce to work together. The Commerce CAO also stated that while he oversees the department's budget as the CFO, he uses his CAO role to look at whether components have demonstrated a sound acquisition management approach in evaluating their budget requests. He also stated that if he were only the agency CAO he would not have as much authority in other functional areas to effectively manage the agency's acquisition function.

- Likewise, the CAO at DHS said that he has oversight of many different management functions such as finance, budgeting, human resources, as well as acquisition. While this arrangement may appear to be in conflict with the statutory requirement that acquisition management be the CAO's primary duty, he stated that having a larger area of responsibility gives him a fuller view of the entire acquisition cycle from requirements development and contract funding to service delivery. As a result, he reports that he spends a majority of his time on acquisition management issues because integrating the different management functions has a positive impact on the CAO's ability to effectively manage acquisitions across DHS.

Almost All CAOs Are Positioned at Top Management Levels

While the SARA legislation does not specify where CAOs should be located within their agency's organization, as shown below in figure 2, we found that almost all of the 16 CAOs were positioned at their agency's top management levels, reporting to either to the agency head or to an official one level removed from the agency head. The CAO at Energy reports to the Director of the Office of Management, who is more than one level removed from the agency head.

Figure 2: Organizational Placement of CAOs

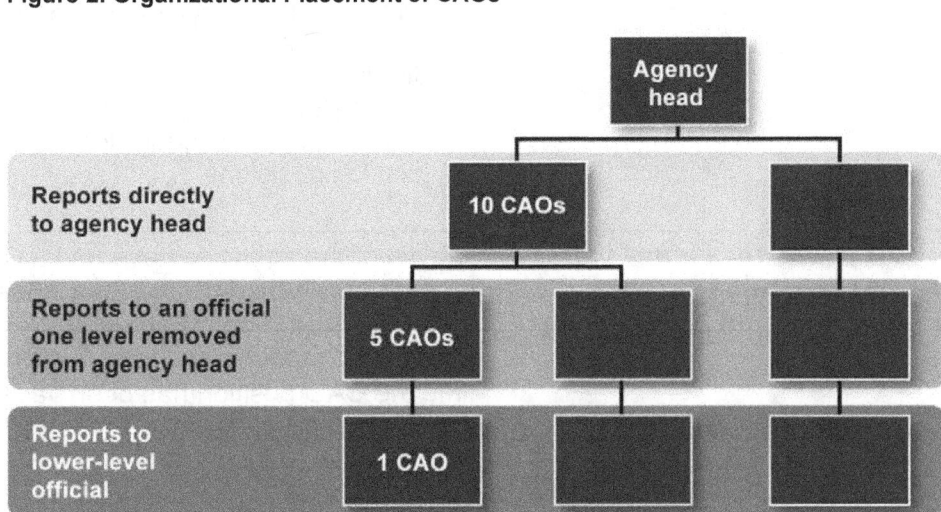

Source: GAO analysis of CAO survey and agency organizational charts.

The location of CAOs at high levels within their agencies may be by virtue of their official titles described above in table 2 rather than being specifically related to the CAO position. Nevertheless, several CAOs and acquisition officials we met with stressed the value of the CAO position in having access to agency leadership and other peers in ensuring that acquisition issues are being considered at top levels within the agency.

- Fourteen CAOs reported that they had at least sufficient access to their agency head, and that the CAO position was appropriately located for ensuring proper authority over their agency's acquisition activities.
- Acquisition officials at the Department of Energy, where the CAO position has been vacant for several years, and whose questionnaire response noted that the CAO had neither sufficient nor insufficient access to the agency head, said that it would have been helpful to have a political appointee in the CAO role who could have high level interactions with agency leadership, better communicate acquisition related issues, and build effective working relationships with the CFO, CIO, and other senior agency officials.
- Additionally, acquisition officials with the Department of the Interior noted that as a political appointee, the CAO can work closely with other assistant secretaries in the department as well as with peers at

other agencies and OMB. They added that with the CAO placed at the assistant secretary level, the position can be more focused on strategic decisions, and can make final decisions on how resources will be deployed to achieve goals.

- Similarly, the HHS CAO said that by virtue of her position, she is able to interact as a peer with the leaders of the agency's operating divisions and communicate the acquisition priorities of the agency and administration. She added that being CAO affords her a "seat at the table" to discuss acquisition issues when the agency is making mission decisions.

CAO Position Usually Filled by Permanent Official, but Tenures Have Been Short

Twelve of the agencies have had a CAO serving in a permanent capacity more than two-thirds of the time since enactment of SARA, as shown below in figure 3. Education and VA have had a CAO serving in a permanent capacity less than 50 percent of the time.[13] The remaining time the CAO position has been vacant or held by an official in an acting capacity.

---

[13] While VA's current CAO is a career official serving in an acting capacity, VA has sought to establish an Assistant Secretary for Acquisition, Logistics, and Construction who would serve as CAO in accordance with the SARA legislation requirements.

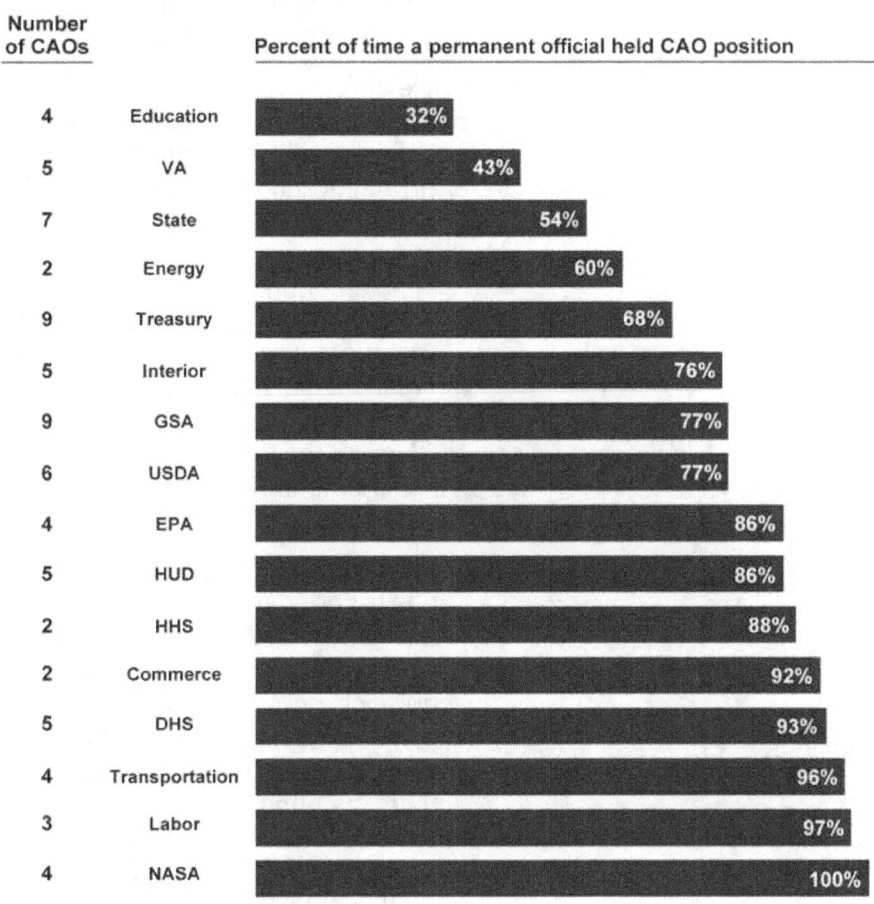

Figure 3: CAO Turnover and Proportion of Time CAO Position Filled by a Permanent Official (from SARA Enactment through April 2012)

Number of CAOs		Percent of time a permanent official held CAO position
4	Education	32%
5	VA	43%
7	State	54%
2	Energy	60%
9	Treasury	68%
5	Interior	76%
9	GSA	77%
6	USDA	77%
4	EPA	86%
5	HUD	86%
2	HHS	88%
2	Commerce	92%
5	DHS	93%
4	Transportation	96%
3	Labor	97%
4	NASA	100%

Source: GAO analysis of agency CAO tenure information.

- Despite most agencies' ability to fill the position with a permanent CAO, turnover in the CAO position varied among agencies, as evidenced by the number of acting and permanent CAOs in place since SARA's enactment. Half of the agencies have had four or fewer CAOs in place, while other agencies have had higher turnover in the CAO position. For example, GSA and Treasury have each had nine CAOs in place since creation of the CAO requirement. The high turnover at GSA and Treasury equate to an average tenure for each CAO of about 10 months at GSA and about 11 months at Treasury since late 2003. In contrast, Commerce and HHS have had only two CAOs over the same timeframe, with an average CAO tenure at each agency of more than 3.5 years.

- Since enactment of SARA, the average tenure of permanent CAOs has been 2.1 years. This is fairly consistent with a recent GAO review that found an average tenure of about 2.6 years for CIOs at 30 federal departments and agencies.[14]

While short tenures in the CAO position may be expected given the political nature of the position, this may work against an individual CAO's ability to effectively implement needed changes in the acquisition function or new acquisition initiatives:

- Our prior work has noted that it can take 5 to 7 years to fully implement major change initiatives in large public and private sector organizations and to transform cultures in a sustainable manner, yet frequent turnover of political leadership in the federal government can make it difficult to obtain sustained attention to make needed changes.[15]
- Among the 76 permanent and acting CAOs that have been in place since the enactment of SARA, only 3 served in the position for 5 years or more.

CAO Involvement in Acquisition Management Functions Varies

CAOs reported they have differing levels of involvement in the management of their agency's acquisition activities. For example, most CAOs indicated they were extremely or very involved in managing acquisition policy, but only somewhat or not at all involved in making acquisition decisions or conducting acquisition assessments. Generally, CAOs saw their role as providing high-level oversight of the acquisition function as opposed to day-to-day management, for which they typically relied on the Senior Procurement Executive and other senior procurement officials. Many CAOs told us that the amount of their involvement is related to several factors, such as the nature of goods and services that the agency buys and the extent the agency has a centralized or decentralized acquisition function. For example, in some agencies, CAOs are less involved because agency units and bureaus operate more autonomously with respect to acquisition management. Our review of

---

[14] GAO, *Federal Chief Information Officers: Opportunities Exist to Improve Role in Information Technology Management*, GAO-11-634 (Washington, D.C.: Sept. 15, 2011).

[15] GAO, *Major Management Challenges and Program Risks: A Governmentwide Perspective*, GAO-03-95 (Washington, D.C.: Jan. 2003); and *Results-Oriented Cultures: Implementation Steps to Assist Mergers and Organizational Transformations*, GAO-03-669 (Washington, D.C.: July 2, 2003).

acquisition regulations and policies found that the roles and responsibilities of the CAO position are not described in detail across all the 16 agencies within the scope of our review. Without clearly defined roles and responsibilities within each federal agency, it will be challenging for these agencies to more permanently institutionalize the CAO position within their organizational structure and realize the benefits from the added attention it brings to acquisition management.

CAO Involvement in SARA Acquisition Management Functions Varied with Most CAOs Focused on High-Level Acquisition Oversight and Policy Management

The SARA legislation broadly outlined acquisition management functions for CAOs and left it up to each agency how to implement them. Overall, CAOs reported varying levels of involvement in the various acquisition management functions we reviewed, as shown below in figure 4:

Figure 4: Level of CAO Involvement in the Eight Acquisition Functions Outlined in SARA Legislation and OMB Guidance

CAO responsibilities	Extremely or very involved	Moderately involved	Somewhat or not at all involved
Monitoring and evaluating agency acquisition activities	7	5	4
Increasing the use of full and open competition	7	4	5
Increasing performance-based contracting	6	4	6
Making acquisition decisions	4	4	8
Managing agency acquisition policy	9	2	5
Acquisition career management	7	4	5
Acquisition resources planning	7	2	7
Conducting acquisition assessments under OMB A-123	4	4	8

Source: GAO analysis of CAO survey.

- CAOs reported being most involved in managing the direction of acquisition policy and least involved in two activities—making acquisition decisions and conducting assessments of the acquisition function under OMB Circular A-123.
- Only three CAOs (Agriculture, Labor, and DHS) reported being extremely or very involved in all eight acquisition management functions.

GAO-12-792 Chief Acquisition Officers

- In contrast, officials at four agencies (Education, Energy, HUD, and State) who were either serving as the acting CAO, recently appointed as the new permanent CAO, or serving as the senior procurement official while the CAO position was vacant, reported being somewhat or not at all involved in seven or more of the acquisition management functions.

Many CAOs see their role as providing high-level acquisition oversight rather than the day-to-day acquisition management that is more typically provided by other career procurement officials such as the Senior Procurement Executive and heads of contracting activities. As shown below in figure 5, a majority of CAOs reported that they delegate day-to-day responsibility for all eight CAO acquisition management functions to the Senior Procurement Executive and/or other senior procurement officials such as heads of contracting activities and competition advocates. The SARA legislation does not preclude CAOs from delegating these functions, and it is not surprising that there is a high degree of delegation given that CAOs have other significant management responsibilities and few had extensive prior experience in acquisition management.

Figure 5: Delegation of Responsibilities Reported by CAOs across the Eight Acquisition Management Functions Outlined in SARA Legislation and OMB Guidance

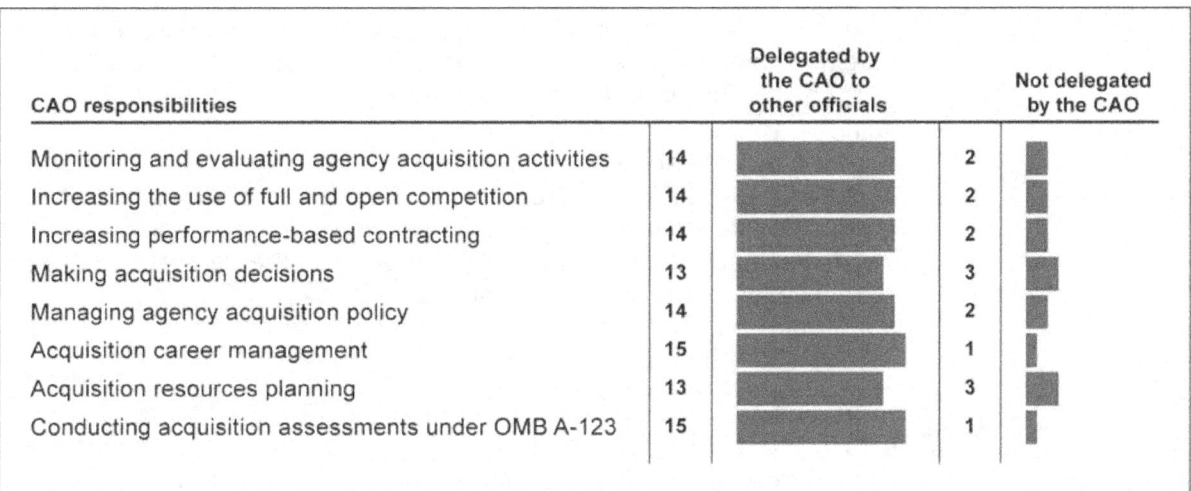

CAO responsibilities	Delegated by the CAO to other officials		Not delegated by the CAO	
Monitoring and evaluating agency acquisition activities	14		2	
Increasing the use of full and open competition	14		2	
Increasing performance-based contracting	14		2	
Making acquisition decisions	13		3	
Managing agency acquisition policy	14		2	
Acquisition career management	15		1	
Acquisition resources planning	13		3	
Conducting acquisition assessments under OMB A-123	15		1	

Source: GAO analysis of CAO survey.

Several CAOs we met with stated that they delegated acquisition management functions to others to ensure that these duties are performed by highly experienced procurement officials. Additionally, they could focus on other acquisition issues such as program management and rely on the agencies' acquisition professionals to manage the agency's contract award process and acquisition workforce.

- For example, the DHS CAO reported delegating seven of the eight CAO acquisition management functions to the Senior Procurement Executive and others, and said that he must take a larger view of the acquisition function that includes program management while the Senior Procurement Executive is more focused on the contract award process and management of contracting officers and contracting specialists.

CAOs' delegation of their responsibilities may also be expected given the roles of other agency officials in acquisition management.

- The Senior Procurement Executive position had been in place at federal agencies for many years before the CAO position was established. This position is typically filled by a career employee who is responsible for the management direction of the agency's procurement system, including implementation of agency unique procurement policies, regulations, and standards.[16]

- In addition, while increasing the use of full and open competition is one of the CAO responsibilities outlined in SARA, each executive agency is also required to designate a competition advocate who is responsible for promoting full and open competition, among other things.[17]
- Similarly, CAOs are responsible for acquisition career management, but the Office of Federal Procurement Policy also requires civilian executive agencies to designate an acquisition career manager who is responsible for, among other things, managing the development and identification of the acquisition workforce and providing input regarding short term and long term human capital strategic planning for the acquisition workforce.[18]

CAO Involvement in Acquisition Management May Vary Due to Agency Characteristics and Other Attributes

CAOs we spoke with stated there is no "one-size fits all" solution for how best to structure the CAO position and integrate the acquisition management responsibilities outlined by SARA. Many CAOs emphasized that the level of acquisition management oversight they provide is based upon several factors, which include the nature of the goods and services that the agency buys and the amount of decentralization in the agency's acquisition function.

- For example, the CAO at HHS said that she is very involved in acquisition policy issues but the oversight of day-to-day acquisition management issues is handled by other officials because much of what HHS buys through contracts is done to support their operating divisions rather than acquisitions of major systems.
- The CAOs at both HHS and Interior reported that their agencies have a decentralized acquisition management structure where heads of operating divisions and bureaus execute most acquisition authority within their two agencies. HHS also stated that although the CAO does not approve acquisition decisions, acquisition management is achieved through the CAO's roles in financial management,

---

[16] 41 U.S.C. § 1702(c).

[17] 41 U.S.C. § 1705 and Federal Acquisition Regulation §§ 6.501and 6.502.

[18] Office of Federal Procurement Policy, *Developing and Managing the Acquisition Workforce* (Washington, D.C.: Apr. 15, 2005).

performance measurement, and acquisition and grants policy and accountability.

In comparison, several CAOs at other agencies play a greater role in the acquisition process. These agencies also tended to have major acquisition programs and projects.

- The CAO at DHS reported having approval authority for individual acquisitions and since assuming the position in 2010 has revised the acquisition oversight structure. The CAO stated that these changes in the oversight structure at DHS are intended to decrease acquisition program risk and provide better insight into budget, schedule and performance information for approximately 135 major acquisition programs for which the CAO serves as the Acquisition Decision Authority.
- CAOs at other agencies who said they are more involved in acquisition management also reported having some form of decision authority over certain acquisitions. For example, the CAO at Commerce serves as co-chair of the agency's Investment Reviews, which provide oversight, review, and advice to the Secretary and Deputy Secretary on both information technology (IT) and non-IT investments that meet certain criteria. This advice includes recommendations for approval or disapproval of funding for new systems and investments, or major modifications to existing systems or investments.
- Similarly, at the Department of Labor, a Procurement Review Board recommends to the CAO approval or disapproval of various acquisition decisions that meet certain thresholds or conditions and serves as a senior-level clearinghouse to review proposed noncompetitive acquisitions.

CAO Roles and Responsibilities Not Clearly Defined at Many Agencies

At many agencies, the CAO position was not clearly defined in documents that would form the basis for more permanently institutionalizing the CAO within their organizational leadership structure. Clearly defined roles and responsibilities for each stakeholder in the acquisition process is a key element of an effective acquisition function, as outlined in GAO's framework for assessing the acquisition function within federal agencies.[19] We found that the amount of detail on a CAO's agency-specific authorities and responsibilities varies greatly based on

---

[19] GAO-05-218G.

the agency's Federal Acquisition Regulation (FAR) supplement and other policy documentation we collected. As shown in table 3, at some agencies, the CAO position is described in detail while for others the only information about the CAO's authorities and acquisition management responsibilities under SARA is a passing reference to the legislation that established the position.

Table 3: Summary of Observations on CAO Position in Agency Acquisition Regulations and Policies

Agency	Defined in agency FAR supplements or acquisition manual	Some or all statutory responsibilities are listed in policy documentation	Neither defined nor statutory responsibilities listed in policy documents
Agriculture			X
Commerce	X		
DHS		X	
Education	X	X	
Energy			X
EPA		X	
GSA		X	
HHS			X
HUD			X
Interior	X		
Labor	X	X	
NASA			X
State			X
Transportation	X		
Treasury			X
VA	X	X	
Totals	**6**	**6**	**7**

Source: GAO analysis of agency acquisition regulations and other policy documentation.

- For example, the CAO position is defined or designated in FAR supplements or acquisition manuals by just 6 of the agencies.
- Detail on the CAO's specific acquisition management responsibilities was listed in other policy documentation for only 6 of the agencies.
- At 7 agencies, the CAO position is not defined in their FAR Supplement or acquisition manual, nor are the acquisition management responsibilities listed in other policy documentation.

GAO-12-792 Chief Acquisition Officers

Additionally, we found that agencies varied in how their acquisition policy guidance delegates authority for procurement matters with respect to the CAO. At half of the agencies, authority for procurement matters is delegated from the agency head through the CAO position to other agency officials. In contrast, at the other 8 agencies, this authority is delegated from the agency head directly to other agency officials such as the Senior Procurement Executive and/or bureau heads, bypassing the CAO. This may be due to agencies neglecting to update their acquisition policies and regulations since creation of the CAO position or to reflect a more recent organizational change.

- For example, the GSA Organizational Manual still refers to an Office of the CAO that reports to the Administrator, which, according to the CAO in place during our review, did not reflect the organizational reporting structure in the agency.

This lack of fully defined CAO roles and responsibilities, and at some agencies, outdated policies, may be an obstacle to ensuring that the CAO position is more permanently institutionalized within the agencies' acquisition management and senior leadership structures.

CAOs Reported Few Significant Challenges and Generally Did Not Identify Changes Needed to Improve Their Effectiveness

CAOs at the 16 agencies generally did not report facing significant challenges related to the CAO position, such as the level of influence they have in their agency's acquisition process, amount of control over acquisition budget resources, and access to agency leadership. However, most CAOs reported that not having enough staff to manage acquisitions was moderately to extremely challenging. As GAO and others have reported in recent years, the capacity and capability of the federal government's acquisition workforce to oversee and manage contracts has been a challenge. Most CAOs did not believe any changes were needed to improve their effectiveness and also felt that they had the appropriate degree of authority to effectively fulfill their acquisition management functions.

Aside from the Sufficiency of Acquisition Staff, CAOs Reported Few Significant Challenges

We asked agency CAOs to indicate how much six management and resource issues that we identified challenged them in carrying out their responsibilities. As shown below in figure 6, CAOs generally answered that most areas we identified were not challenges for them.

Figure 6: Extent of Challenge Reported by CAOs in Fulfilling Their Acquisition Management Responsibilities

Challenge areas	Extremely or very challenging		Moderately challenging		Somewhat or not at all challenging	
Level of influence in agency's acquisition process	1	▮	5	▬	10	▬▬
Amount of control over acquisition budgetary resources	3	▬	3	▮	9	▬▬
Sufficiency of staff to manage acquisitions	6	▬▬	5	▬	5	▬
Employment status of CAO (career vs. appointed)	0		0		15	▬▬▬
Sufficiency of access to agency leadership	0		2	▮	14	▬▬▬
CAO position turnover	1	▮	0		13	▬▬▬

Source: GAO analysis of CAO questionnaire responses.

Note: Responses in some challenge areas do not sum to 16 because "Not Applicable" or "Don't Know" responses are not included.

- No CAOs reported being very or extremely challenged by their employment status (career official versus political appointee) in fulfilling their acquisition management functions or in having sufficient access to agency leadership.
- The CAOs at DHS, HHS, and State reported five of these areas as being not at all challenging. In contrast, the CAO at GSA and the career acquisition official at Energy reported being moderately to extremely challenged in most of the areas.

Despite the lack of challenges reported by CAOs related to most areas, 11 CAOs reported the sufficiency of staff to manage acquisitions as a moderate to extreme challenge. These responses echo concerns from our prior work that the capacity and the capability of the federal government's acquisition workforce to oversee and manage contracts have not kept pace with increased spending for increasingly complex purchases. Additionally, 6 of the 16 agencies' IGs have identified the acquisition workforce as a source of serious management challenge in their most recent management challenge reports issued during 2011. However, none of the CAOs at these 6 agencies reported the sufficiency of acquisition staff as extremely or very challenging.

Majority of CAOs Said No Additional Changes Needed to Improve Their Effectiveness

When asked if any other changes were needed to improve their effectiveness, 10 out of 16 CAOs reported that no changes were needed. Six CAOs did provide some suggestions. For example, Energy's response to our questionnaire stated that the CAO position needs improved resource support and full engagement with the agency's senior leadership team. At EPA, the CAO responded that it would be helpful if there were a better understanding of the contracting process by agency management. The GSA CAO, who left the position during our review, believed that returning the CAO position to a direct report to the GSA Administrator would improve the position's effectiveness at her agency. Following the completion of our CAO questionnaire, GSA appointed an Acting CAO who reports to the Acting GSA Administrator. CAOs at Transportation, Interior, and HUD reported that more budgetary resources and acquisition workforce staff are needed to improve their effectiveness. Despite these responses and other issues raised in our report, almost all the CAOs believed that they had the appropriate authority to fulfill their acquisition management responsibilities.

Conclusions

More than 8 years after the enactment of the SARA legislation, there is wide variation in how agencies have implemented the CAO position. On one hand, agencies have generally filled the CAO position with political appointees who sit at relatively high levels within their agencies in a position to ensure that acquisition is receiving attention from agency leadership. Many CAOs and acquisition officials we met with cited this as a key benefit of the CAO position. On the other hand, there are inconsistencies in the implementation of the law across agencies, with very few CAOs having acquisition management as their primary responsibility, although many CAOs cited the benefits to integrating acquisition management with their additional responsibilities. The CAO position is only one factor of many in an efficient, effective, and accountable acquisition function in agencies. Having an experienced Senior Procurement Executive is another. There is no one-size-fits-all approach to how to organize an effective acquisition function, and a CAO's role should be suited to the nature and volume of an agency's acquisition activities. Yet, agencies should ensure that they are maximizing their chances for success by having CAOs that are in a position to influence agency leadership and serve as a strong advocate for acquisition management, which includes having clearly defined roles and responsibilities for the CAO. Not all agencies have these, however, and may be missing an opportunity to ensure that the CAO position is fully institutionalized within agencies' acquisition management and senior leadership structures. Given CAOs' short tenures, a lack of defined roles and responsibilities could hinder a CAO's ability to maximize time in the position and serve as an effective advocate for acquisition management.

Recommendation for Executive Action

To strengthen the functions of CAOs in acquisition management, we recommend that the Administrator of the Office of Federal Procurement Policy, working with the CAO Council, issue guidance to agencies directing them to ensure that CAO roles and responsibilities are more clearly defined in accordance with law and regulations, tailored to suit the agency's acquisition activities, and documented as appropriate.

Agency Comments and Our Evaluation

We sent copies of a draft of this report to OMB and the 16 agencies within the scope of our review. OMB's Office of Federal Procurement Policy provided comments via e-mail, in which it concurred with our recommendation. The office also suggested that the report further highlight the role of the Senior Procurement Executive in providing day-to-day leadership of an agency's acquisition function. We considered this suggestion and made changes to the report as appropriate.

We received communications from each of the 16 agencies, with 15 providing no substantive comments. HHS provided additional information on the roles and responsibilities of the CAO, which we incorporated into the draft. HHS's written comments are reproduced in appendix III.

We are sending copies of this report to other interested congressional committees, the Director of the Office of Management and Budget, and the Secretaries of Agriculture, Commerce, Education, Energy, Health and Human Services, Homeland Security, Housing and Urban Development, the Interior, Labor, State, Transportation, the Treasury, and Veterans Affairs; the administrators of the Environmental Protection Agency and the National Aeronautics and Space Administration, and the Acting Administrator of General Services. In addition, this report will be available at no charge on the GAO website at http://www.gao.gov.

If you or your staff have any questions concerning this report, please contact me at (202) 512-4841 or by e-mail at woodsw@gao.gov. Contact points for our Offices of Congressional Relations and Public Affairs are on the last page of this report. Key contributors to this report are listed in appendix IV.

William T. Woods
Director, Acquisition and Sourcing Management

Appendix I: Objectives, Scope, and Methodology

Our objectives were to assess: (1) how agencies have filled the Chief Acquisition Officer (CAO) position; (2) the extent to which CAOs are involved in performing the acquisition management functions set forth in the Services Acquisition Reform Act of 2003 (SARA) legislation and Office of Management and Budget (OMB) guidance, and (3) what challenges, if any, agency CAOs report in fulfilling their responsibilities for acquisition management. Our review did not assess the effectiveness of individual CAOs or individual agencies' acquisition functions.

To address our objectives, we reviewed the SARA legislation and directives from OMB's Office of Federal Procurement Policy to identify the key roles and responsibilities of the CAO position. We also reviewed previous GAO work on assessing the acquisition function and the implementation of other chief officer positions in the federal government. To learn more about CAOs' characteristics, as well as CAOs' involvement in acquisition management functions and challenges faced in fulfilling their responsibilities, we developed and administered a questionnaire by e-mail in an attached Microsoft Word form to the 16 civilian agencies[1] within the scope of our review.[2] We pretested the questionnaire to ensure that the questions were relevant, clearly stated, and easy to understand. We also solicited comments on the draft questionnaire from members of the Chief Acquisition Officers Council. The questionnaire requested information on, among other things, the CAOs' reporting relationships, involvement in acquisition management functions within the agency, the

---

[1] We sent the questionnaire to the Departments of Agriculture, Commerce, Education, Energy, Health and Human Services, Homeland Security, Housing and Urban Development, the Interior, Labor, State, Transportation, the Treasury, Veterans Affairs, the Environmental Protection Agency, the National Aeronautics and Space Administration, and the General Services Administration (GSA).

[2] SARA required executive agencies described in certain sections of the Chief Financial Officers Act of 1990, Pub. L. No. 101-576 (see, 31 U.S.C. §§ 901(b)(1) and 901(b)(2)(C) (CFO Act)), to appoint a CAO. When SARA was enacted in 2003, the U.S. Code listed GSA under 31 U.S.C. § 901(b)(2)(C). In 2004, the Department of Homeland Security Financial Accountability Act, Pub. L. No. 108-330, § 3, amended the CFO Act to make a number of changes, including adding the Department of Homeland Security to the list of agencies required to have a CFO and changing GSA's position on the CFO list. For the purposes of this report, we included GSA in our review, as it was listed in section 901(b)(2)(C) of title 31 of the U.S. Code when SARA was enacted. The SARA legislation exempts the Department of Defense (DOD) from the CAO requirement. Legislation enacted prior to SARA required DOD to have an Under Secretary of Defense (Acquisition, Technology & Logistics) who has responsibilities similar to those of a CAO. Justice is not required to appoint a CAO under the SARA legislation, but has designated the Assistant Attorney General for Administration as the CAO.

extent to which the CAO had delegated their acquisition management
responsibilities to other officials, and challenges identified by GAO that
CAOs may have experienced in fulfilling their responsibilities. We sent the
questionnaire to agencies in November 2011. All questionnaires were
returned by March 2012. We received responses from all 16 agencies,
though not all agencies provided responses to each question.

To provide additional information on CAOs' characteristics, involvement in
acquisition management functions and challenges faced, as well as to
corroborate information provided in the questionnaire responses, we
collected and reviewed agencies' organizational charts that showed the
CAO's position relative to the head of the agency and other senior
officials; letters of delegation or other documents that formally designate
the appointment of the CAO, the CAO's resume or curriculum vitae
describing their qualifications and experience related to the CAO position;
applicable policies, guidance, position descriptions or functional
statements for both the CAO and Senior Procurement Executive
positions; applicable policies or orders that delegate the CAO's
responsibilities to other acquisition officials; agency acquisition function
assessments performed under OMB Circular A-123; Acquisition Human
Capital Plans or similar documents; agency strategic plans and
performance reports; agency-specific acquisition regulations and
acquisition manuals; and descriptions of acquisition metrics or
performance measures the agency tracks. We also asked each agency to
supply the name, time in office, and circumstances (whether they were in
an acting or permanent position and whether they were a career
employee or political appointee) of each of the individuals who had
served as agency CAO and Senior Procurement Executive since
enactment of the SARA legislation in November 2003.

To complement information gathered through the questionnaire and
agency documentation, we conducted follow-up interviews to discuss the
CAO's roles and responsibilities with CAOs and acquisition officials at
seven agencies: Commerce, Department of Homeland Security (DHS),
Department of Health and Human Services (HHS), Interior, Energy, GSA,
and the National Aeronautics and Space Administration (NASA). We used
a nongeneralizable sample of agencies based upon the following criteria:
review of the questionnaire responses, the amount of procurement
spending as a portion of the agency's fiscal year 2010 budget, and
whether the agency's Inspector General had identified acquisition-related
issues as a major management challenge. We also met with officials from
OMB's Office of Federal Procurement Policy to discuss the roles and
responsibilities of agency CAOs.

We conducted this performance audit from October 2011 to July 2012 in
accordance with generally accepted government auditing standards.
Those standards require that we plan and perform the audit to obtain
sufficient, appropriate evidence to provide a reasonable basis for our
findings and conclusions based on our audit objectives. We believe that
the evidence obtained provides a reasonable basis for our findings and
conclusions based on our audit objectives.

CAO responsibility	Source	Description
Monitoring and evaluating agency acquisition activities	SARA legislation	Monitoring the performance of acquisition activities and acquisition programs of the executive agency, evaluating the performance of those programs on the basis of applicable performance measurements, and advising the head of the executive agency regarding the appropriate business strategy to achieve the mission of the executive agency
Increasing the use of full and open competition	SARA legislation	Increasing the use of full and open competition in the acquisition of property and services by the executive agency by establishing policies, procedures, and practices that ensure that the executive agency receives a sufficient number of sealed bids or competitive proposals from responsible sources to fulfill the Government's requirements at the lowest cost or best value considering the nature of the property or service procured.
Increasing performance-based contracting	SARA legislation	Increasing appropriate use of performance-based contracting and performance specifications
Making acquisition decisions	SARA legislation	Making acquisition decisions consistent with all applicable laws and establishing clear lines of authority, accountability, and responsibility for acquisition decision-making within the executive agency
Managing agency acquisition policy	SARA legislation	Managing the direction of acquisition policy for the executive agency, including implementation of the unique acquisition policies, regulations, and standards of the executive agency
Acquisition career management	SARA legislation	Developing and maintaining an acquisition career management program in the executive agency to ensure that there is an adequate professional workforce
Acquisition resources planning	SARA legislation	As part of the strategic planning and performance evaluation process, assessing the requirements established for agency personnel regarding knowledge and skill in acquisition resources management and the adequacy of such requirements for facilitating the achievement of the performance goals established for acquisition management; developing strategies and specific plans for hiring, training and professional development to rectify any deficiency in meeting such requirements; and reporting to the head of the executive agency on the progress made in improving acquisition management capability.
Conducting acquisition assessments under OMB A-123	OMB Memorandum for Chief Acquisition Officers, May 21, 2008, Conducting Acquisition Assessments under OMB Circular A-123, Guidelines for Assessing the Acquisition Function	Conducting entity-level internal control reviews of the acquisition function under OMB Circular A-123

Source: GAO analysis of SARA legislation and OMB memorandum.

Appendix III: Comments from the Department of Health and Human Services

DEPARTMENT OF HEALTH & HUMAN SERVICES

OFFICE OF THE SECRETARY

Assistant Secretary for Legislation
Washington, DC 20201

JUL 1 3 2012

Bill Woods, Director
Acquisition and Sourcing Management
U.S. Government Accountability Office
441 G Street NW
Washington, DC 20548

Dear Mr. Woods:

Attached are comments on the U.S. Government Accountability Office's (GAO) report entitled, "Chief Acquisition Officers: Appointments Generally Conform to Legislative Requirements, but Agencies Need to Clearly Define Roles and Responsibilities" (GAO-12-792).

The Department appreciates the opportunity to review this report prior to publication.

Sincerely,

Jim R. Esquea
Assistant Secretary for Legislation

Attachment

**GENERAL COMMENTS OF THE DEPARTMENT OF HEALTH AND HUMAN
SERVICES (HHS) ON THE GOVERNMENT ACCOUNTABILITY OFFICE'S (GAO)
DRAFT REPORT ENTITLED, "CHIEF ACQUISITION OFFICERS: APPOINTMENTS
GENERALLY CONFORM TO LEGISLATIVE REQUIREMENTS, BUT AGENCIES
NEED TO CLEARLY DEFINE ROLES AND RESPONSIBILITIES" (GAO-12-792)**

The Department appreciates the opportunity to comment on this draft report entitled, "Chief
Acquisition Officers: Appointments Generally Conform to Legislative Requirements, but
Agencies Need to Clearly Define Roles and Responsibilities" (GAO-12-792). HHS concurs
with the overall findings of the draft report, and offers the following comments:

- As noted in the report, the HHS Senior Procurement Executive (SPE) does not report
  directly to the Chief Acquisition Officer (CAO), which at HHS is the Assistant Secretary
  for Financial Resources (ASFR). Rather, the Senior Procurement Executive reports to
  the Deputy Assistant Secretary (DAS) for Grants and Acquisition Policy and
  Accountability. Although this provides, organizationally, an indirect relationship
  between the CAO and the SPE, the CAO delegated acquisition authority directly to the
  SPE and since the SPE falls within the CAO's chain of command, the two are able to
  communicate frequently on the Department's acquisition policies, priorities, and
  programs. Additionally, the DAS role enables the CAO to align and manage the
  Department's grants and acquisition priorities, policies, and oversight activities.

- With regard to the CAO's involvement in Acquisition Management, the Department
  reiterates that the HHS CAO is very involved in acquisition policy issues, as well as the
  implementation of the various acquisition-related priorities. The day-to-day conduct of
  the acquisition function is delegated by the CAO to the heads of HHS's operating
  divisions, and in turn to the ten Heads of Contracting Activity at HHS. The
  Department's acquisitions, including those for major acquisition programs or systems, are
  managed at the agency-level to support the mission of each operating division. Even
  though the Department does not formally use the CAO to approve acquisition decisions,
  as is done at other Departments, acquisition management is achieved through her roles in
  the Department's budget formulation and execution, financial auditing and reporting,
  performance measurement, and acquisition and grants policy and accountability.

We appreciate GAO's efforts under this report to share its observations of the CAO function at
other Departments, which HHS can learn from.

1

Appendix IV: GAO Contact and Staff Acknowledgments

GAO Contact	William T. Woods, (202) 512-4841 or woodsw@gao.gov
Staff Acknowledgments	In addition to the contact named above, John Oppenheim (Assistant Director); Matthew Drerup; Kristine Hassinger; Lauren Heft; Jean McSween; Roxanna Sun; and Robert Swierczek made key contributions to this report.

GAO's Mission	The Government Accountability Office, the audit, evaluation, and investigative arm of Congress, exists to support Congress in meeting its constitutional responsibilities and to help improve the performance and accountability of the federal government for the American people. GAO examines the use of public funds; evaluates federal programs and policies; and provides analyses, recommendations, and other assistance to help Congress make informed oversight, policy, and funding decisions. GAO's commitment to good government is reflected in its core values of accountability, integrity, and reliability.
Obtaining Copies of GAO Reports and Testimony	The fastest and easiest way to obtain copies of GAO documents at no cost is through GAO's website (www.gao.gov). Each weekday afternoon, GAO posts on its website newly released reports, testimony, and correspondence. To have GAO e-mail you a list of newly posted products, go to www.gao.gov and select "E-mail Updates."
Order by Phone	The price of each GAO publication reflects GAO's actual cost of production and distribution and depends on the number of pages in the publication and whether the publication is printed in color or black and white. Pricing and ordering information is posted on GAO's website, http://www.gao.gov/ordering.htm. Place orders by calling (202) 512-6000, toll free (866) 801-7077, or TDD (202) 512-2537. Orders may be paid for using American Express, Discover Card, MasterCard, Visa, check, or money order. Call for additional information.
Connect with GAO	Connect with GAO on Facebook, Flickr, Twitter, and YouTube. Subscribe to our RSS Feeds or E-mail Updates. Listen to our Podcasts. Visit GAO on the web at www.gao.gov.
To Report Fraud, Waste, and Abuse in Federal Programs	Contact: Website: www.gao.gov/fraudnet/fraudnet.htm E-mail: fraudnet@gao.gov Automated answering system: (800) 424-5454 or (202) 512-7470
Congressional Relations	Katherine Siggerud, Managing Director, siggerudk@gao.gov, (202) 512-4400, U.S. Government Accountability Office, 441 G Street NW, Room 7125, Washington, DC 20548
Public Affairs	Chuck Young, Managing Director, youngc1@gao.gov, (202) 512-4800 U.S. Government Accountability Office, 441 G Street NW, Room 7149 Washington, DC 20548